SERVICE LEARNING FOR TEENS™

WORKING WITH VETERANS AND MILITARY FAMILIES
THROUGH SERVICE LEARNING

ANN BYERS

ROSEN
PUBLISHING®

New York

Published in 2015 by The Rosen Publishing Group, Inc.
29 East 21st Street, New York, NY 10010

Copyright © 2015 by The Rosen Publishing Group, Inc.

First Edition

Library of Congress Cataloging-in-Publication Data

Byers, Ann.
Working with veterans and military families through service learning/
Ann Byers.—First edition.
        pages cm.—(Service learning for teens)
Includes bibliographical references and index.
ISBN 978-1-4777-7963-7 (library bound)
1. Service learning—United States—Juvenile literature. 2. Veterans—
Services for—United States—Juvenile literature. 3. Families of military
personnel—Services for—United States—Juvenile literature.
LC221.B94 2014
361.3'7—dc23

                                                                    2014012524

Manufactured in the United States of America

On the cover: Army chaplain (Capt.) Roger Benimoff (*left*) offers counseling and guidance to Sgt. Andrew Buchanan, a twenty-five-year-old veteran from Iraq who lost part of his ankle in an IED blast. Veterans can always use the help of civilians as well. There are ample opportunities for teens to reach out and make contact with veterans in their communities and offer help and assistance that can greatly improve the lives of those who served and their families.

CONTENTS

Introduction   4

CHAPTER ONE
Service Learning: A Double Win   7

CHAPTER TWO
Backing the Front   22

CHAPTER THREE
Strengthening the Back   34

CHAPTER FOUR
We Won't Forget   43

CHAPTER FIVE
Getting Started   57

Glossary   67
For More Information   69
For Further Reading   72
Bibliography   74
Index   78

Can a student in a school in the United States make a serious difference in a war half a world away? The answer is definitely *yes!* One story from a soldier in Iraq illustrates the life-saving influence a student can have. The Stuffed Animals for Emergencies website posted the story from letters the soldier sent to his parents:

American marines regularly patrolled streets in Iraq's most dangerous cities, trying to keep them safe for the men and women who lived and worked there. They were saddened by the sight of children who had few material possessions and often seemed frightened by the foreigners with their Jeeps and their guns. How could the marines show the children that the Americans were their friends?

Back in the United States, students were also concerned about the boys and girls in Iraq. They had researched what was happening in that country. They were aware of the continuing struggle for peace and security. They knew that many of the children were traumatized by the fighting they had witnessed and the suffering they were still experiencing. What could the students do to help the American military help the Iraqi children?

A U.S. marine, looking for enemy soldiers in a city in Iraq, stops to give a teddy bear to a small Iraqi girl.

The answer to both questions came in the form of a classroom project. In the course of their research, the students found AdoptaPlatoon, an organization that encourages individuals and groups in the United States to support men and women serving in the military overseas by sending them materials they request. One of the items the marines in Iraq asked for was children's toys. Adopta-Platoon partnered with another organization, a group that collects and sends stuffed animals to comfort children who are hurting. Through the classroom project, boxes of soft toy animals arrived at a marine base in Iraq.

Before the marines patrolled the streets, they filled their big pockets with the stuffed toys from the students. Whenever they came across children, they stopped their vehicles and offered them the animals. The delighted children hugged the toys and smiled back at the Americans.

The marines did not always have animals or other gifts to give. On one occasion, when they were patrolling with empty pockets, a small child sat in the middle of the road, blocking their path. The girl would not move, so the convoy started to swerve slowly around her. One of the marines recognized the stubborn child—she held a fuzzy bear he had given her on a previous patrol. Thinking she might remember him, the marine stopped the line of Jeeps and knelt down to talk to her. She looked frightened but relieved to see a familiar face. She pointed to a spot not far away, and the marine recognized a roadside mine. He lifted the child to safety, cordoned off the area, and had the device deactivated.

Not every service project has such a dramatic result. But every time someone engages in service for a good cause, positive things happen for both the one being served and the person who is serving. That is just one reason service learning involving military families and veterans is such an exciting venture.

CHAPTER ONE

SERVICE LEARNING: A DOUBLE WIN

The armies and battlefields of the twenty-first century are a far cry from those of the past. By the same token, the classrooms of today are not like the schoolrooms of yesterday. The difference is more than the presence of smartboards, laptops, and electronic tablets. Schools are using more interactive, practical, and diverse ways of engaging students. One increasingly popular educational practice is service learning. As the name implies, service learning combines some type of helpful work in the community (service) with academic growth (learning).

IT'S ABOUT LEARNING

Service learning is, first and foremost, about learning. Teachers have always encouraged their students to become involved in service, and students usually learn something in the process. But service learning goes beyond having students participate in a project and asking them what they learned. Service learning uses service projects to help students gain the knowledge and skills they are supposed to learn at their particular grade level. Its primary purpose is to help students learn school subjects, develop academic skills, and grow in their ability to become productive citizens.

Take as an example the project in which students sent stuffed animals to troops in Iraq. What subject matter did they learn? They read about the history of the country, the different ethnic and religious groups, the way the government and society functioned, and how the leaders and the people responded to events in the region. They examined the influence of culture, religion, and relationships with other countries on daily life. If they traced the route of the stuffed animals from their collection to their destination, they learned some of the geography of the Middle East and parts of the United States. These are all parts of the social studies standards they are expected to know.

What academic skills did the students develop? They did a variety of writing. They composed letters and announcements explaining their project, asking for donations, and thanking their donors. They tucked notes and letters to the military in with the toys.

Learning where places are in the world is easier and more fun when students have a personal interest in the geography they study.

They might have also documented their activities in journals, reports, and school newsletter articles. The students honed their math and calculation skills as they kept track of incoming monetary donations and outgoing costs for repair and cleaning of items, shipping materials, postage, and other expenses. They learned to plan, schedule, and organize all the activities involved in soliciting, sorting, packing, and sending the stuffed animals.

IT'S ABOUT SERVING

Service learning is first about learning, but it is also about serving. In traditional methods of teaching, students learn facts, but the facts may be completely unrelated to anything else in their lives. When learning is irrelevant, students are often not excited about what they are learning and they don't remember the facts for long. But incorporating serving into learning makes the learning meaningful. Knowing the names of some soldiers in a foreign country makes people more interested in what those soldiers are doing there. When collecting toys for children affected by war, you want to understand what the fighting is about and what daily life is like for the children. Service projects motivate students to learn. They connect what happens at school with what is going on in the world around them.

Incorporating service into learning also makes learning rewarding. When one learns facts, the reward is a good grade. When one not only learns facts but also serves someone in the process, one feels a sense of satisfaction. Making a positive difference for another

Before they can serve, students must research a problem. They have to apply language, math, social science, and critical-thinking skills.

person boosts self-confidence and self-esteem. It develops understanding, empathy, and respect for other people.

To qualify as service learning, a project has to meet a real need, so it has to be bigger than picking up the trash on school grounds. The service has to have some kind of meaningful effect on the people it serves. The Iraq project example addressed two needs: The marines needed to build good relationships with the Iraqi people, and the children were without toys. Ideally, a service-learning project connects students with people in their community who provide ongoing service. The students in this example partnered with AdoptaPlatoon and Stuffed Animals for Emergencies, Inc.

BONUS LEARNING

With service projects, students gain far more than mastery of subject matter. The kind of organization required to carry out a service-learning project develops skills that cannot be taught in a traditional lecture format. These include interpersonal skills, such as communicating effectively and getting along with others, and the critical thinking skills of analyzing, evaluating, predicting, reasoning things out, and solving problems. The best way to develop these skills is by using them in real-life situations.

Because service-learning projects involve the community beyond the students' family and school, they help students develop citizenship skills and values. Students acquire positive attitudes about justice, diversity, responsibility, conservation, and other issues that make them good citizens. In sending stuffed animals to children in war-torn Iraq, students learned to understand and respect a culture different from theirs. They developed a concerned attitude for people who were suffering, an appreciation for the duties and ability of the military, and an understanding of how to win trust. They learned that

A SCHOOL PROJECT GOES GLOBAL

It's impossible to gauge just how far a service project might reach. Shauna Fleming was a fifteen-year-old freshman in Orange, California, in 2004. She heard about some of the hardships plaguing American soldiers during and after their service overseas. She also heard that receiving letters from people at home lightened some of the burden for them. That's when she went to her principal and proposed a service project: a campaign to send a million thank-you letters to a million service men and women. She called it A Million Thanks.

She kicked off her project with a school assembly. Some local television stations brought their cameras, and the story was picked up by a national wire service. It made its way across the country and into the *Armed Forces Press.* People began sending letters and cards to Shauna to forward to Iraq and Afghanistan, and military platoons sent names of soldiers. Shauna reached her goal of one million thanks in seven months.

But she didn't stop there. A Million Thanks now has a website, sponsors, partners, teams of volunteers, and drop-off boxes in twenty-five states. Shauna has added a second project: Wounded Soldier's Wish. Its purpose is to raise funds to fulfill some of the dreams of men and women who were wounded in service to their country. Meanwhile, the campaign that began as a high school service project has sent more than six million thank-yous from grateful Americans of all ages...and still counting.

they could make a difference in helping solve a large problem, and they experienced the pride and satisfaction that comes with doing something that matters for someone else.

In addition to these benefits, service-learning projects often have extra learning opportunities that have to do with the specific project. In this project, students learned what an in-kind donation is and how nonprofit

The U.S. Postal Service has a variety of options for mailing letters and packages. Understanding the different methods and choosing the best one can be part of service learning.

organizations credit donations for tax purposes. They learned the postal regulations for preparing and sending packages overseas. They also got a feel for career fields they may never have otherwise considered: military, postal, nonprofit management, and fund-raising.

HOW IT WORKS

What makes service learning so powerful is that the students make many of the decisions about how it will work. Teachers guide them, of course, but the students design and carry out the service project. Teachers keep them on track, but students drive the efforts in each of service learning's five parts: investigation, planning, action, reflection, and demonstration.

Service learning begins with a problem—a real-world problem that is connected with curriculum standards. For example, one of the learning objectives of the National Council for the Social Studies is that students can explain "how experiences may be interpreted differently by people from diverse cultural perspectives and frames of reference." The very real conflict between different groups in Iraq certainly provided opportunities for meeting this standard. The teacher presents students with the problem and the students investigate the issue and consider how the problem might be solved or lessened.

In the planning stage, the students have to use critical thinking skills to analyze possible solutions, evaluate whether they might work, and predict the likely outcomes of specific actions. They explore organizations that are already working to meet the need and select groups with which they can partner and specific actions that are realistic for them. They come up with a project, and then the logistic planning begins. What are the steps needed to carry out the project? How much time will the project take? What will it cost? Do they have the time, money, other resources, and the manpower to complete it? The students, not the teacher, plan the details of the project. For instance, in our example, how would the students find the stuffed animals? Would they simply ask friends and family? Would they put notices in the school newspaper? Would they partner with an elementary school, church, or club with younger children? Would they ask stores for donations? What about public service announcements on the radio or television? Would they use social media?

After the planning is done, students begin the action phase, actually performing the service. Think of the different tasks involved in the example:

- Ask people to donate stuffed animals
- Establish collection points where people take their donations
- Thank donors
- Provide receipts
- Clean and repair used animals
- Write letters to the soldiers and/or children to go with the toys
- Pack the animals according to postal and military regulations

- Raise the money needed for mailing packages overseas
- Meet the requirements of the partnering organizations

Each task is the responsibility of the student or student team.

REFLECTION

The teacher's main responsibility, once the students settle on a project, is to guide them in reflecting on their activities. Reflection is what makes an activity a learning experience. Reflection connects the experience with the learning goals. It is the difference between knowledge and understanding. Reflection enables students to clarify their thoughts and feelings and gain insight about the new information they are acquiring.

Reflection must take place at every stage of service learning. During investigation, planning, and serving, teachers have students stop and think about what and how they are learning. They go deeper than asking, "What did you learn?" They ask, "Why does this matter? How does it relate to what you already know? How does it relate to anything else in your life? How has it changed you? What difference has it made to someone else?"

Class discussions are just the beginning of reflection. Students can keep journals, recording what they are doing and what they are thinking and feeling about what they are doing. Teachers can assign essays,

Thinking about the real-life effects of their real-world actions enables students to grasp the practical meaning of the subjects they are studying.

having students compare what they knew and thought about their topic before and after the project. They can post their activities and thoughts about them on a school blog, invite comments from other students, and respond to those comments.

DEMONSTRATION

The greatest form of reflection comes at the end of the project. That is the time for the students to demonstrate what they have done and learned. As in the investigation, planning, and action stages, the students direct this phase. They decide how they will show what they accomplished. Remember, they started with a problem; they need to show what difference they made in that problem. A good demonstration has some before and after comparison. In the Iraq example, part of the "before" could be pictures and numbers of the children in Iraq displaced from their homes by war; "after" could be an accounting of the number of children who received stuffed animals as a result of the project. Any

A bulletin board displaying information about a project is one form of demonstration. It can be an art, language, or computer graphics activity as well as a social studies task.

thank-you letters students receive from the soldiers or from partnering organizations show the project's positive influence. A good demonstration also shows how the project changed the students.

The possibilities for demonstration are many: verbal presentations to other classes, to school faculty, and to parent or community groups. Posters, bulletin boards, or other art projects displayed in prominent locations. Photos and reflections posted on the school's website. Demonstration of learning is a time for celebration, and not just for the students. A successful service-learning project touches the community, and the community often joins in the celebration.

Service learning offers many and varied possibilities for students. Service can be direct—working closely with the people served—or indirect—providing support from a distance. Whether direct or indirect, there are many opportunities for service learning with military families and veterans.

CHAPTER TWO

BACKING THE FRONT

Service-learning projects must meet real needs, and military life presents plenty of needs. The majority of the men and women in the armed services are stationed outside the United States, in more than 150 countries. They are in combat, training foreign armies, or guarding American embassies. Some provide support to the ones in harm's way; others gather intelligence. Many, even those who are not in war zones, have dangerous assignments.

Most of those overseas are without their families, some for long periods of time. They miss important events, such as the birth of a son or daughter. They face the uncertainties of an unfamiliar and sometimes hostile environment. Those in combat zones deal with the added pressures of having to always stay on guard, with distrust on all sides, of being in the midst of violence and suffering. They also cope with physical hardships: periods with too little food, water, and sleep; sore feet and aching muscles; and perhaps extreme heat or cold.

This army sergeant from New Jersey was serving in Afghanistan on Christmas day. A letter from home brightened his holiday.

These are the problems. What are the solutions? What could make their situations better? Receiving specific items they need is helpful. So is opening a package of "comfort items": treats they don't actually need but really enjoy. As simple as it sounds, just hearing from people at home can brighten a soldier's day. Even when those people are strangers, their letters, cards, and gifts let the military know that they are not forgotten. Those packages tell them that the people for whom they are enduring hardships appreciate their sacrifice.

LETTERS GO A LONG WAY

Almost everyone, even young children, can send a card or a letter of thanks. Do those letters really matter? Yes, they do, judging from some of the responses received by A Million Thanks, one of many organizations that coordinate shipments of letters to the military:

- "Your support has significantly raised the morale of our marines. It's people like you that keep the marines motivated and proud to serve our country."
- "I was shot during a firefight . . . [and had] to have my left leg amputated just above the knee. I have chosen to continue my service and return to Iraq because of support such as yours."
- "Being 5,000 miles away from home is difficult. These cards make us feel like we have families everywhere... Support from the home front keeps our soldiers in the right mind-set to stay focused on their missions."

Sending letters and cards is one of the easiest service-learning projects possible; even an elementary school class can carry it out. Third-graders in Massachusetts persuaded their entire school (kindergarten through grade 7) to write letters and create cards. In addition to sharpening their English, writing, and art skills, they used their math skills to sort the five hundred letters for mailing to different groups in different locations: soldiers in Afghanistan, sailors in the Atlantic, airmen in the Middle East, and soldiers in Europe. Many organizations are available to arrange the details of getting the messages to the troops.

LITTLE PIECES OF HOME

Older students might want to go a step further, collecting and sending materials that are in short supply on military bases. Think of some of the toiletry items everyone runs out of at their houses: shampoo, soap, and toothpaste, for instance. Soldiers and sailors run out of these things, too. Military bases may not stock enough deodorant, dental floss, or razors. Over the course of a long deployment, some essentials can also wear out. There seems to always be a need for socks and underwear.

Providing necessities is important, but military personnel also appreciate the extras. A package containing cookies, energy bars, and candy or gum are little reminders of home they cannot get overseas. They also welcome diversions for their downtimes: CDs and DVDs, magazines, puzzle books, and hand-held games.

A number of organizations facilitate shipment of packages, and they supply lists of suggested items. They also list what they cannot send, including aerosol cans, hand sanitizer, glass containers, and home-baked goodies. Some concentrate on specific types of items.

A mother-daughter team organized the Southern Illinois Yellow Ribbon Campaign in 2003. They send thousands of donated items to soldiers every year.

The Hugs Project sends cool ties and warm hats. Books for Soldiers, Magazines for Troops, and DVDs4Vets provide entertainment. Operation Foot Care Patrol supplies foot care kits containing nail clippers, socks, creams, and powder. Service learners have many great partnering opportunities.

COOL HUGS

It began when Karen Stark sent a letter to a marine in Iraq. Soon she and her husband were writing letters to some of his friends. After a while, they started to send care packages with the letters. Then Karen read a heartbreaking story about a young woman who had died of heatstroke while standing guard duty. At about the same time, a random article appeared in her e-mail. It described how to sew cool ties—small, thin scarves that can lower body temperature 7 degrees. Stark couldn't sew very well, so she asked for help on an Internet message board. The response overwhelmed her; dozens of people offered to make the ties and send them overseas. She could see the ties hugging soldiers' necks like loving embraces, and she named her venture the Hugs Project.

Today, more than three thousand people in every state and fifty-eight foreign countries sew cool ties and send them to military bases. The project has expanded to include helmet coolers (which Stark calls "kisses") and hats, scarves, and gloves for winter. The project also sends hats, small bears, and backpacks for the troops to distribute to children. Everything is handmade; Karen Stark supplies patterns through Yahoo! groups. Everything, especially the hugs, is made with love.

It is important to choose an organization at the beginning of a service-learning project and follow that organization's guidelines. These organizations know what the recipients need, and they can provide lists that include items that might be surprising, such as insect repellant wipes. They are very handy in hot climates, as are sunscreen and lip balm. Dust cloths are especially welcome in sandy deserts, and one of the most requested items is baby wipes.

BACKING THE MISSION

One way to serve the military is to support their mission. A big part of their current mission is to rebuild nations devastated by wars and disasters. That means training their armies, repairing roads and bridges, digging wells where there is no running water, and constructing schools and libraries. It means healing their wounded, caring for their poor, and building goodwill among their citizens.

This is a need that is ideal for service learning. Instead of (or in addition to) sending soldiers items for their own use, students might ship materials the soldiers can distribute to the people they are trying to help. Hospitals that have been damaged need medical supplies, schools need books and educational tools, and citizens who have lost their homes, need clothing and household items. Common items such as paper, pencils, and toys are treasures for people who are trying to rebuild their lives. Some of the groups that send packages to the military partner with organizations that provide these types of items.

Another way of backing the mission is to raise funds for these organizations. Raising funds develops planning, organization, and communication skills. Three students at a charter school in Minnesota used a service-learning assignment to support an organization that establishes schools, trains teachers, and provides humanitarian aid to Afghanistan. The students asked local business owners to let them place donation jars in their offices and stores and invite employees and customers to give toward the project. They contributed hundreds of dollars to Help the Afghan Children and helped the American soldiers in Afghanistan build good relationships with the children there.

Students raising funds for a service-learning project should not disregard small donations. Elementary students in Colorado raised more than $800 for soldiers in two weeks by collecting donations of change.

HELP THEM CONNECT

For troops thousands of miles from home, one of the greatest needs is to stay connected with loved ones. Some are deployed for many months and over

Robbie Bergquist and his sister have collected millions of cell phones for soldiers through their organization, Cell Phones for Soldiers.

holidays, and they miss their families. Calling from overseas is very expensive. Again, this is a problem a service-learning project can meet.

The Cell Phones for Soldiers organization collects unused cell phones, recycles them, and uses the proceeds to purchase prepaid phone cards that deployed military can use where they are stationed. It also has a program for purchasing no-longer-used iPhones directly from individuals and reselling them, converting the profit into calling cards. The organization welcomes student partners. Students can organize drives to collect phones, set up collection sites, get the phones to the organization, and facilitate sales of iPhones.

A small group of students in Ventura, California, partnered with Cell Phones for Soldiers and their local army recruiting station in a service-learning project. They made banners and posters to solicit donations at their school, and they collected more than two hundred phones and $100. Their work and that of many others was greatly appreciated, as this letter from a soldier to the organization shows: "Of all of the items that we get from the caring people at home, these calling cards are probably the best. While I do like a box full of snacks in the mail, nothing beats being able to talk to my wife and son back home."

FOUR-FOOTED SOLDIERS

When thinking of military service, canine units might not immediately come to mind. Dogs are important military assets, guarding bases, searching buildings, and sniffing out bombs. For some troops in active

This navy dog handler is preparing his dog, Argo, for service in Iraq. A bomb and patrol dog, Argo will sniff out bombs and people and apprehend enemy soldiers.

war zones, they are an indispensable, first line of defense against enemy soldiers and improvised explosive devices.

Life on the front line is difficult for the dogs, especially when the front line is in a desert. When the thermometer climbs as high as 140° F (60° C), the animals cannot cool off, and they tire in an hour or two. The blistering sand and asphalt burn their paws. Even a slight breeze blows hot sand into their eyes. This might be another problem ripe for a service-learning project.

There are organizations that supply materials that make the dogs' job easier. Support Military Working Dogs sends cooling vests, doggles for their eyes, muttluks for their paws, and mutt muffs to protect their ears when they ride in helicopters. U.S. Wardogs packages some of the same items, as well as grooming supplies and food for the canine soldiers. Vest-A-Dog and Kevlar for K9s send bullet-proof vests. Students can research how dogs are trained and used by the military, what types of care and equipment they require, and what happens to retired service animals. They can partner with one of these organizations to meet some of the needs of the four-footed soldiers.

CHAPTER THREE

STRENGTHENING THE BACK

Even when stationed in the United States, military families have challenges. Because they are assigned to different locations, they move more than most families. Their children typically attend six to nine schools by the time they graduate. The frequent relocations not only drain their finances, but also take them away from extended family and friends who could provide support.

When the service person is deployed overseas, the challenges grow. Living without a spouse, parent, or child for months on end is difficult under any circumstances. Knowing that a loved one is likely to be performing strenuous and dangerous tasks in harsh surroundings makes the separation even harder. Many families receive few letters and even fewer phone calls. They live with the ever-present stress of wondering how and if their loved ones will return. These families need support; they need to know that people understand their hardships and care about them. They need to be able to forget their fears and worries for a time.

Sometimes the person who is absent is someone everyone in the family depended on. Perhaps it is the mom, who cooked, did the shopping, and had the main responsibility for caring for the children. Maybe it is the dad, who kept the car tuned up, mowed the lawn, and repaired everything around the house. Or it could have been the son or daughter who took care of aging parents or grandparents. In these cases, those left behind need some practical help. A great service-learning project would be to identify local military families, find out what they need, and help them meet those needs.

FILLING THE GAPS

If a military or guard base is nearby, it should be easy to discover ways to serve military families. There is usually a family resource center, family support center, or other department on the base that is in contact with families. If no military facility is close by, try locating military families through veterans' service organizations. The Department of Veterans Affairs publishes a list of these organizations. Through these contacts it's possible to find a wife who needs a fence painted, a mother who just gave birth, a father who had surgery and would appreciate hot meals, or a child who could use tutoring or special attention. Direct service-learning projects can fill the gaps created by deployment.

One of the needs of families of deployed military is a break from the stress of their everyday lives. According to a study by the RAND Corporation, the spouses and children of deployed military have higher levels of anxiety than others, and the longer the deployment, the greater the stress. Any event that would replace the worries with fun, even for a short time, would be welcome.

Some communities near military bases offer regular or occasional recreational opportunities for the men and women stationed at the bases and their families. For example, a marine base and an air force base are not far from Lake Havasu City in

Service-learning projects often involve fund-raising. Selling home-baked goods is one way to raise money and also involve the community in the project.

Arizona. The city hosts weekends for the marines and airmen and women, treating them to boat rides on the lake, jet skiing, excursions into the desert, barbecues, concerts, and other entertainment. It might be possible to piggyback on such an event for a service-learning project, putting on a pancake breakfast, distributing home-cooked goodies, or organizing a volleyball tournament or other games. If the community does not do anything like that, think about trying to get something started.

TAP INTO YOUR PASSIONS

The children of deployed military, like any children, would welcome any fun and attention you give them,

Serving children in military families does not require specific skills. Just taking a child for a bike ride helps fill the void left by a deployed parent.

and their parents undoubtedly appreciate anything positive you can add to their children's lives. The best ways to serve children is to tap into your talents or interests. Good athletes might put together a softball team, conduct a soccer camp, or teach karate. They could enlist sporting goods suppliers as partners. If art is a strength, craft stores

> YOU CAN HEAR THEM NOW!

How old does someone have to be to make a big difference across the globe? In 2004, Robbie and Brittany Bergquist were twelve and thirteen years old, respectively, when they encountered an Iraq veteran. He had come home with a phone bill that totaled almost $8,000. As young as they were, the brother and sister knew a little something about phones, particularly cell phones. Cell phones can be refurbished and sold again. Or they can be taken apart and their plastics and metals used for other products. Either way, Robbie and Brittany knew there was money in discarded phones. They wondered if that money could be put toward keeping the troops from racking up huge bills when they called home.

They found a way. With only $21, they began a drive to collect cell phones that were not being used, sell them to recyclers, and use the money to buy minutes. The minutes could be placed on calling cards that soldiers could use from landlines anywhere in the world. Recycling just one phone yields about two and a half hours of free talk time.

It was a small beginning, but it grew into a huge operation. In its first ten years, the Bergquists have recycled more than 11 million phones and given away over 204 million minutes. They have received numerous awards, but the prizes of which they are proudest are the many letters they receive from grateful soldiers.

or local artists might help present a creativity workshop. Ideas for activities with children are practically limitless: an afternoon making puppets, a board game night, a sewing class, a beauty workshop, or a day shooting and editing videos. Turn whatever you like to do into a tool for serving kids.

That is exactly what Kate Stansbury did in Rocky Point, New York. One of her passions was swimming, so she partnered with a swim school in her city to provide free swimming lessons to children of military families. She advertised the offer in the military community, wrote lesson plans for the instruction, coordinated the lessons with the children's schedules, and acted as a lifeguard during the lessons.

INDIRECT SERVICE

Another student put her passion into practice in indirect service. Emily Newton lived in Fayetteville, North Carolina, near the headquarters of Operation Kid Comfort. An "army brat" herself, Emily knew the need children of military have for comfort when a parent is far away. She volunteered at the organization.

Operation Kid Comfort makes photo-transfer quilts for children. They are made with photographs that family members send in of their deployed loved ones. Volunteers scan the images, edit them, and print them on fabric. They combine the pictures with other pieces of donated material and stitch them into beautiful quilts. The quilts are then sent, at no charge, to the children, who cherish the photos of their parents.

Emily began at age ten, just sorting the pieces of fabric. By the time she was fourteen, she was not only an expert at quilting, but she was also teaching adult volunteers and organizing quilting events. Although Emily's contribution to children of the military was not a service-learning project, it illustrates what someone can do and give to another organization.

Supporting the work of a good organization is a valuable service-learning project, especially when direct service is not possible. Often, the action component of service learning consists of planning and conducting fund-raisers for groups that provide the direct benefit. For example, students exploring the impact of deployment on children might decide to raise funds for an organization called Dog Tags for Kids. This organization makes dog tags like those the servicemen and women wear, in the colors of each branch of the armed forces. The tags are engraved "With Love

A military wife holds a photo-transfer quilt that belongs to her daughter. She has become a volunteer, starting a chapter of Operation Comfort in Augusta, Georgia.

from Dad (or Mom)" above the name of the branch and the place of deployment. They are shipped to the various locations and the soldiers, sailors, marines, or airmen or women mail them home to their children. This gives the children something from dad or mom that they can wear or hold onto until their parent returns.

Two college students in Parma, Ohio, found a way to serve military families overseas. Caitlyn and Maria Toth learned that commissaries on overseas bases accept manufacturers' coupons that expired within the past six months. Since military families are often on tight budgets, coupons that enable them to purchase items

Sending coupons that offer savings on purchases not only help military families financially, but also reminds them that people at home have not forgotten them.

for a little less are very helpful. The girls partnered with two American Legion Ladies Auxiliary posts and the organization Coupons to Troops. They used a website and Facebook to ask people to donate coupons. Because the coupons were delivered directly to people who asked for them, they knew their project made a positive difference for military families.

SPUR OTHERS TO ACTION

Some military families have needs beyond a student's ability to meet. Some people may need transportation to doctors' appointments or the grocery store, assistance filling out paperwork, or help with home repairs. A service-learning project might help these families. If a classroom cannot meet the needs, perhaps it's possible to find adults who can. Consider surveying adult friends and family and making a list of what skills and services they are willing to provide. Contact plumbers, roofers, and people in other trades and ask if they would be willing to donate some of their time. Partner with a club or church to find people. This project would be a clearinghouse that gathers information and matches people to needs. It would be necessary to set up a system for connecting the military families in need with the adults who can help them. Don't forget to publicize to the families the fact that the services you are collecting are available. Even families that never request any of the services will be encouraged by knowing that the people of their community stand behind them, ready to lend a hand if necessary, and support what their loved ones are doing for them.

CHAPTER FOUR

WE WON'T FORGET

When soldiers end their service, they often come home with wounds and scars. The physical wounds are obvious and often severe. Advancements in medical technology mean that soldiers are surviving injuries that would have been deadly not many years ago, but their recovery is often long and difficult. Many veterans learn to function without an arm or leg, without sight or hearing, or with constant pain. Their wounds make many simple tasks of daily living difficult, if not impossible.

Many more veterans deal with invisible wounds. Probably at least half of all military returning from combat experience post-traumatic stress (PTS). They feel anxious and depressed, and some

These three soldiers are among many who lost limbs in wars in the Middle East. Playing basketball is part of their rehabilitation.

consider suicide. The psychological scars frequently interfere with their relationships and make reconnecting with their families a challenge. The violent behaviors and defensive reactions they were forced to use in war do not work in civilian life and adjusting is difficult. Unemployment and homelessness among veterans are considerably higher than in the general population.

These problems are not short term or easily solved. A number of veterans of the Vietnam War that ended forty years ago are still coping with physical and psychological scars. But just as notes of appreciation, packages of comfort items, and practical assistance ease the suffering for active-duty soldiers and their families, there are ways to make the problems of veterans less severe.

REMEMBER THE WOUNDED

If a veterans' hospital is nearby, there are great opportunities for individual service-learning projects. The Department of Veterans Affairs (VA) has a student volunteer program and encourages people sixteen and older to get involved. The department provides training and placement in a wide variety of medical and social work specialties.

A Martinsburg, West Virginia, student discovered what she wanted to pursue as a career by volunteering in a VA hospital. Christiana Hess served in the pharmacy department for two years. She told a *Herald Mail* reporter, "When I watched them provide personal care to the veterans... I saw myself doing the same work.

Young hospital volunteers relax between duties. In addition to work in medical fields, veterans' hospital teen volunteers can serve in food service, social work, information technology, administration, and medical illustration.

It's through volunteering that I know I want to become a pharmacist and to continue serving our veterans." A bonus that Christiana received because of her volunteering will help her achieve her goal: a $20,000 scholarship the VA awards to outstanding youth volunteers. Another reward may be just as meaningful to her. She said, "I never realized how much I could impact a person's life until I volunteered."

> FOR THE FAMILIES OF THE FALLEN

At first, it was just a way to honor a friend. When Phil Taylor's friend died on the battlefield of Iraq, he expressed his sorrow to the soldier's family in the only way he could think of: he painted his picture. Phil was an artist by profession, painting commissioned portraits of celebrities. So he made a picture of his friend, smiling proudly in his military uniform. According to the American Fallen Soldiers Project website, when he presented his gift, his friend's father's reaction stunned him. "I feel like you've brought him home to me," he sobbed. At that moment, Phil understood how much the gift meant to a grieving parent. The portrait showed that someone cared, that the soldier was not forgotten. It brought honor to the hero and his sacrifice and comfort to those who missed him. The artist resolved that he would give that same gift to as many Gold Star families as he could.

Through his nonprofit organization, American Fallen Soldiers Project, Phil receives donations that enable him to paint and present as many as forty portraits a year to families who have lost loved ones to war. He examines multiple pictures and talks with family to understand the soldier's story and personality. Each picture takes 60 to 120 hours to paint. Unless the family requests something more private, Phil presents the framed 24 × 30-inch (61 × 76-centimeter) portrait in a public ceremony to give further honor to the fallen soldier.

A service-learning project does not have to take two years to have an impact. A group of high school students in Chula Vista, California, found that a one-time contact with veterans can leave a lasting impression. The students made cards and baked cookies and bread, and took them to wounded sailors at nearby Balboa Naval Hospital. Student Gabi Marks told Beth Zimmerman of Pets for Patriots, "This trip was definitely a life-changing experience I will never forget. It was so humbling to thank our wounded warriors, and saddening to see how young most of them are... I am always humbled by these veterans who have sacrificed so much for our freedom."

REMEMBER THE DEEDS

Because veterans have sacrificed so much for such an important cause, they do not want their deeds to be forgotten. Since 2000, the U.S. Library of Congress has been collecting and preserving records of those deeds, and its program offers great service-learning opportunities. The Veterans History Project gathers letters, diaries, photographs, and other materials from and about American war veterans, but its main concern is capturing the veterans' stories. Collections of stories are called oral history, and the Veterans History Project is primarily an oral history project.

The American Folklife Center of the Library of Congress invites adults and students in grades 10 and above to interview veterans and submit audio and/or video recordings of their stories to the project. The center provides a list of suggested questions and samples of completed interviews. For students who may

be doing a service-learning project, the center gives additional guidelines and some resources for background information. It supplies everything but the veterans.

Sixteen-year-old Andrew Layton, a student in Battle Creek, Michigan, found veterans at a local VA hospital. In documenting the story of a World War II Medal of Honor recipient for the Veterans History Project, Andrew developed interviewing, writing, and computer technology skills. He perfected those skills in his next project: recording the stories of fifty-six World War II flying aces from Michigan and compiling then into a book.

A class at the Bronx Lab School incorporated interviewing into their service-learning project, but they did not gather oral histories. The problem they examined was the issues facing current veterans. To

Two students interview a veteran. Teaming up on interviews usually stimulates more questions and gets more information. It also enables students to discuss what they learned.

find veterans, they researched possible partnering organizations, an important element in service-learning projects. They settled on Iraq and Afghanistan Veterans of America, an organization with an office not far from the school. Prior to the interviews, the students divided up into four teams and researched four issues faced by veterans: physical disabilities, PTS, unemployment and homelessness, and the GI bill that determines the benefits veterans receive. They developed their own interview questions and videotaped the interviews. Each team combined the interview footage with other images to produce a film describing the veterans' issue. The end product consisted of four short films with a wealth of information.

Between the World War II vets and the veterans of today's conflicts is a large group that was largely ignored until somewhat recently: veterans of Vietnam. The Vietnam Veterans Memorial Fund has created a service-learning opportunity that remembers the deeds of these servicemen and women. The organization built a memorial wall on the National Mall in Washington, D.C., that has the names of fifty-eight thousand service members who died in the war. The organization would like to add photographs and stories to a display in the visitor center next to the Wall. It has created a curriculum and resources for a Hometown Heroes

service-learning project, asking students to identify victims and veterans of the Vietnam War, document their stories, and send all the information they can to the Vietnam Veterans Memorial Fund.

Thousands of people visit the Vietnam Memorial Wall, many searching for names of people they knew. This unnamed veteran salutes one or more of the fallen heroes.

MEET THE NEEDS

Remembering their sacrifices is important to veterans, but addressing their immediate concerns is a more pressing need. One glaring need among veterans is homelessness. The U.S. Department of Housing and Urban Development estimated the number of homeless veterans in 2013 at almost fifty-eight thousand.

A Boston middle school class constructed a service-learning project around this issue. The concern surfaced as the students studied the U.S. Constitution and considered the rights of citizens. To explore the problem, the students served in a veterans' homeless shelter, stocking shelves, sorting clothes, and serving lunch. They interviewed some veterans living in the shelter, as well as several staff who worked there. Combining what they learned at the shelter and in their classroom, they wrote a skit about the Bill of Rights, published a report in a school newsletter, and wrote letters to their congressperson about homelessness among veterans. They performed their skit at the shelter, to the delight of the veterans, their teachers, and the administration of both their school and the shelter. Further, they partnered with the Election Commission and the League of Women Voters to conduct a voter registration drive.

The middle school students saw positive changes in their attitudes toward the homeless, but they could do little to solve the problem for

the veterans. A college class, however, was able to make a dent in the problem. Culinary arts students from Johnson and Wales University in Providence, Rhode Island, partnered with Operation Stand Down

Veterans file through the chow line at the 2013 Stand Down Weekend in Cumberland, Rhode Island. Students served breakfast and lunch to the veterans, who camped in military tents.

in a service-learning project. Operation Stand Down is an organization that coordinates many agencies and groups to bring services to veterans, especially homeless veterans. At a weekend event, veterans have access to counseling, help with housing and job applications, legal advice, information about drug and alcohol recovery programs, and a host of other services. The university students served more than one thousand meals at Stand Down Weekend.

HONOR THE SERVICE

As Stand Down Weekends show, a larger group can offer more service. Some schools combine classrooms for bigger projects. At a high school in North Adams, Massachusetts, twenty-five freshman history students developed a service-learning project to honor veterans at a Memorial Day event. They created a historical exhibit and a slide show with pictures of local military and veterans and images of war monuments. Students from computer and digital media arts classes made a graphic collage that was displayed at the event. Chorus and band students folded their service-learning project into the event. They researched the musical traditions of the military and learned and performed those songs. The finished product, a Memorial Day parade and celebration, was a huge event that sparked excitement and patriotism throughout the entire school and honored the many veterans in the community.

If a school-wide project could generate so much enthusiasm, imagine what an even larger project could accomplish. In 2010–2011, the public school district in Beavercreek, Ohio, had the entire district cooperate in a giant service-learning project. Students in every grade at all the schools learned about citizenship. The district selected for its project raising funds for Honor Flight, the organization that flies war veterans to Washington, D.C., to visit the memorials that honor their service and sacrifice. In each school, students had to decide how to raise their share of the fund-raising goal, which was $10,000—enough to send thirty veterans. The ideas and work all came from the students. From book sales, a pasta dinner, a talent show, a dance modeled on World War II-era servicemen's clubs, and other activities, the students raised $19,500 and sent sixty-three veterans on a trip that many described as the greatest Memorial Day of their lives.

A service project does not have to be huge to bring honor to veterans. A group of scouts in Concord, New Hampshire, noticed that the city's Veterans' Memorial Monument was in disrepair after sixty years of neglect. The scouts put together a plan for its restoration. Partnering with local veterans' organizations and doing all kinds of odd jobs, they raised $3,000. To update the monument, one of the scouts designed five large bronze plaques for the five branches of the service. The boys did most of the physical work of power washing, replacing worn grout, deep cleaning, and adding the plaques. Their only purpose for the project was to honor the service of the veterans for whom it had been originally erected. A marine attending the unveiling of the restored memorial let them know they had achieved their goal. "It stands for something," he told

Even with a power washer, it took many hours of hard work for Boy Scout Troop 90 and its leaders to clean and restore this 1953 veterans' memorial monument.

Jeremy Blackman. "For those guys who never came home… That's what we have to remember them by. So when I see monuments that have been cleaned up, it's a really good feeling." The same can be said about most service-learning projects with veterans: it's a really good feeling.

CHAPTER FIVE

GETTING STARTED

Service-learning projects that focus on the military, military families, or veterans are many and varied. Knowing where to begin, what type of service to offer, and whom to partner with can be a challenge.

Talents and resources are great places to start. Those who like to sew or do needlework can check out the organizations that make hats and scarves for the troops and toys and blankets for children in war-torn areas. Good with a camera? Document the situations of veterans in the community. Students in an art class in Massachusetts used their skills to produce oil paintings and frame photographs to give to low-income veterans to brighten the blank

A number of organizations supply patterns for students to knit or crochet hats, socks, and scarves for the military and sew items for patients in veterans' hospitals.

walls of their rooms. Music or drama students might brainstorm the types of entertainment they could provide to veterans in hospitals or shelters. Those who really enjoy working with children can think about what they could do for the children of military families in their area.

WHO WILL HELP?

Once it has been determined who the project will serve and what you will do, it is time to find organizations to partner with. Groups that provide services to the military and veterans are mentioned throughout this resource and are provided in the websites at the end. Do not overlook local organizations that can help with different aspects of the project.

If the event will involve serving a meal or snacks, contact fast-food restaurants, bakeries, coffee houses, doughnut or bagel shops, dairies, and other businesses that handle food and drinks. Don't stop with just one. Serve sandwiches from a delicatessen, chips from a grocer, apples from a grower, and dessert from an ice cream parlor. Many businesses include donations in their budgets, and they might be happy to help a school and honor the troops at the same time. Make sure to acknowledge their donations to the people attending the event.

Does the project involve printed materials like advertisements, tickets, surveys, or newsletters? Perhaps it involves compiling research into booklets to distribute. Copy shops or office supply stores may be willing to duplicate the materials. If a college or any type of

> BRACELETS THAT SAVE LIVES

Looking for an item to include in care packages for soldiers? Try weaving paracord survival bracelets. Made of super-strong parachute cord, a survival bracelet is a multipurpose emergency tool. The thin cord can withstand 550 pounds (about 250 kilograms) of pressure, more than enough to tie down a tent in a storm or pull an injured person to safety. It is a braided sheath that holds seven to nine inner strands, each fine enough to sew on a button or close up a wound. Paracord bracelets allow service men and women to carry about 8 feet (2.4 meters) of the versatile cord effortlessly wherever they go.

The bracelet saved the life of a sniper in Iraq. A mortar exploded close enough to his position to tear his leg open. He unwound the cord and used it to make a tourniquet. He wrote to Survival Straps, the company that supplied the bracelet, "It's safe to say I might not have made it out without your straps."

This life-saving piece of equipment is inexpensive, easy to make, and lightweight to ship. Instructions for making the bracelet are available from several Internet sites. Most organizations that mail packages to the troops would be glad to tuck a few bracelets in with their other supplies. One organization, Operation Gratitude, has a project devoted to the bracelets. Weaving paracord survival bracelets is a great service project for anyone who is crafty.

A great benefit of service learning is the opportunity to explore new areas and career paths. These teens are developing construction skills while they are serving.

specialty school is nearby, some students might appreciate a little experience in the field they are studying.

Think about the businesses that do anything similar to the project. If it is sports-related, ask sporting goods stores for help. If the project requires collecting and giving away toys, clothing, or books, look to companies that deal in those items. They may have outdated or overstocked merchandise they are happy to offer. For projects that involve building something, talk with managers of hardware stores and lumber-yards. They may be willing not only to supply materials, but to actually get involved in the project, too. Home Depot has a program, Project Homefront, to help military families with home repairs while family members are deployed.

TURNING A NEED INTO A PROJECT

Teachers initiate some service-learning projects, whereas others surface because students see a need. Benjamin Hulett of Shaftsbury, Vermont, had been noticing a need for some time. Every year, his Boy Scout troop joined veterans' organizations and other volunteers in placing flags at the gravesites of veterans in all the cemeteries in the city for Memorial Day. Benjamin found his volunteer service a little challenging because some tombstones were difficult to read. He had a hard time telling whether the stone belonged to a veteran or a civilian. That meant some of the gravesites were missed, and when family members visited on Memorial Day, their loved ones were not honored with a flag.

Benjamin saw the need, and he came up with a solution. Partnering with a chapter of the Veterans of Foreign Wars, American Legion posts, and a local church, he outlined a plan to identify all the graves of veterans. He would purchase small medallions and have them engraved with the words "U.S. Veteran."

He would see to it that every headstone or footstone that marked the resting place of a veteran had one of these medallions clearly visible. Benjamin personally led the fund-raising effort, which was successful. Now no veteran's grave in that city's cemeteries is without a flag on Memorial Day.

THE SERVICE GOES ON

Benjamin's project took months to complete. Many school service-learning projects are not scheduled to last that long. But sometimes, when the learning is over, the project continues because it has worked its way into students' hearts. That is one of the benefits of service learning: it develops in students' compassion for others and a sense of civic responsibility. It can even birth an entire organization that continues the service, as it did for Shauna Fleming and her project, A Million Thanks.

Greg Brown, a sixteen-year-old Jacksonville, North Carolina, student, is discovering how long a commitment to a service project can be. He discovered a need when his friend's stepfather came home from his service overseas without his legs. Among the veteran's many challenges is caring for his lawn. Greg heard him say that that he wished he had a zero-turn mower but he could not afford one.

Greg knows about mowers. He has operated his own lawn care and landscape business since he was eleven. He knows how expensive zero-turn mowers are. But he also understands that being able to mow his lawn by himself would enable his friend's stepdad to regain some of the independence he has lost. Greg thought of a way to help him reach that

Daytona 500 champion Kevin Harvick and the company that co-owns the car he races partnered with Shauna Fleming to encourage people who attend racing events to write letters thanking soldiers.

goal. The teen normally mows five to eleven lawns a week. If he pushes himself, he figures he can knock out thirty in a day. His plan is to set aside a full week, find people who will pay him to mow their yards, and donate all the proceeds to the project. He calculates that he can net about $4,800, almost enough for a zero-turn mower for his friend and one other veteran. He hopes that the company he purchases the machines from will donate a little, too. Long term, he wants to make major lawnmower companies aware of the needs of handicapped people. "My biggest hope," he told Brennan Thomas, "is that they'll come out with a wounded-warrior edition mower."

JUST DO IT

Greg still has not realized all he wants from his project. He didn't know when he started if he would be able to complete it. He had no idea if he could find enough customers, and he wasn't sure if he could actually mow thirty lawns in a day. He had no assurance the lawnmower supplier would help. But two things were important. First, he thought the project through, calculated carefully, and thought the objective was achievable; he didn't tackle more than he believed he could handle or

Greg Brown, age sixteen, is seen here with the riding mower he uses in his lawn care and landscaping business. He saw a need and set about meeting it.

set a goal he couldn't see himself reaching. Second, even though he had no guarantee he could pull off what he planned, he went through with it anyway. Service learning is, after all, about learning, and learning is a process of trial and error. Greg may have to set aside another week to raise more money. He may have to enlist the help of another gardener or two or do something entirely different to raise awareness of the needs of disabled veterans. He might need to have his congressperson approach the lawnmower company. Readjusting his plan is not failure; it is part of learning. Every time students hit a bump in the road toward working their project, they learn something new. When everything comes together and they reflect on how it happened, they also learn. What matters is that they attacked a problem in their community, did something about it, grew academically and personally, and made a positive difference for someone else. That is truly what service learning is all about.

GLOSSARY

brat A child of a member of the armed services.

clearinghouse An agency that collects and distributes information.

commissary A store that sells to military personnel and their families.

commissioned Given an official job. A military officer can be commissioned, and an artist can be commissioned to do a particular work.

cordoned Prevented access to an area by surrounding it with a rope or a line of police or soldiers.

curriculum The subject matter taught in a school at a particular grade level.

deployment Assignment to a place of battle. Troops sent into a combat zone are said to be deployed.

dog tag An identification tag made of thin metal and worn on a chain around the neck.

GI A U.S. serviceman or woman. Technically, it is the acronym for "government issue," meaning provided by an official military supply department.

Gold Star family A family of a military person killed in war. The term originated in World War I, when families displayed blue stars in their windows to indicate a child in the service and a gold star to indicate a fallen soldier.

indirect service Service in which the person serving does not have contact with the person or persons being served.

in-kind donation A donation of an item or service, rather than money.

intelligence Information a government collects, usually secretly, about its enemies.

landline A channel of telephone communication that uses cables or wires laid across land, rather than towers or satellites, which are used by cell phones.

logistic Pertaining to actions that must be taken to complete a complex task.

post-traumatic stress (PTS) A psychological condition that results from extremely stressful experiences. It is characterized by anxiety, depression, nightmares, and flashbacks of the stressful occurrence.

reflection The process of thinking seriously and critically about an experience and its effects and implications.

standard An academic or curriculum standard is a statement of what students at a particular level should know and be able to do and how that performance will be measured.

wire service A news organization that provides newspapers, radio, and television stations with news.

zero-turn mower A riding lawn mower, steered with hand controls, that can turn within a radius of a few inches.

FOR MORE INFORMATION

AdoptaPlatoon
P.O. Box 234
Lozano, TX 78568
Website: http://www.adoptaplatoon.org
AdoptaPlatoon is a nonprofit organization that supports
   American military deployed overseas by conducting
   campaigns, partnering with other groups, and facil-
   itating shipments of materials that encourage and
   support military personnel.

Canadian Alliance for Community Service-Learning
2128 Dunton Tower
Carleton University
1125 Colonel By Drive
Ottawa, ON K1S 5B6
Canada
(613) 520-2600 Ext. 8241
Website: http://www.communityservicelearning.ca
The Canadian Alliance for Community Service-Learning is
   an association of educators that provides research,
   education, resources, advocacy, and networking that
   foster the growth of service learning.

Cell Phones for Soldiers
243 Winter Street
Norwell, MA 02061
(866) 716-2220
Website: http://www.cellphonesforsoldiers.com
Cell Phones for Soldiers is a family-operated nonprofit
   organization that collects and recycles cell phones
   and uses the funds to supply deployed military with
   free telephone calling cards.

Hugs Project
720 W. Wilshire, Suite 105
Oklahoma City, OK 73116
(405) 651-8359
Website: http://www.thehugsproject.com
The Hugs Project is a nonprofit organization with several
chapters and thousands of online members who
make and send cool ties, warm hats, and other items
to military deployed overseas.

National Coalition for Academic Service Learning
1776 Massachusetts Avenue NW, Suite 201
Washington, DC 20009
(202) 775-0290
Website: http://ncasl.org
The National Coalition for Academic Service Learning
is an organization of education professionals who
provide models and resources that promote service
learning.

Support Military Working Dogs
P.O. Box 122
Donnelsville, OH 45319-0122
(937) 308-6950
Website: http://www.supportmilitaryworkingdogs.org
Support Military Working Dogs provides protective gear
for military dogs working in active combat zones
and extreme conditions.

Veterans History Project
American Folklife Center

Library of Congress
101 Independence Avenue SE
Washington, DC 20540-4610
(202) 707-5510
Website: http://www.loc.gov/folklife
The American Folklife Center is a part of the U.S.
Library of Congress. It researches and documents
materials related to American life and traditions,
including oral histories.

Wounded Warriors Canada
310 Byron Street South, Suite 4
Whitby, ON L1N 4P8
Canada
(888) 706-4808
Website: http://woundedwarriors.ca
Wounded Warriors is a nonprofit organization that
helps Canadian armed forces members who have
been injured in their service to Canada and helps
any Canadian veteran in need adjust to civilian life.

WEBSITES

Because of the changing nature of Internet links, Rosen
Publishing has developed an online list of websites
related to the subject of this book. This site is updated
regularly. Please use this link to access the list:

http://www.rosenlinks.com/SLFT/Vete

FOR FURTHER READING

Anderson, Laurie Halse. *The Impossible Knife of Memory.* New York, NY: Viking, 2014.

Bingham, Jane. *The Gulf Wars with Iraq.* North Mankato, MN: Heinemann Raintree, 2012.

Doller, Trish. *Something Like Normal.* New York, NY: Bloomsbury, 2013.

Ellis, Deborah. *Kids of Kabul: Living Bravely Through a Never-Ending War.* Toronto, ON, Canada: Groundwood, 2012.

Engdahl, Sylvia. *Military Families.* Farmington Hills, MI: Greenhaven, 2014.

Fleming, Shauna, and L. A. Stanford. *A Million Thanks.* New York, NY: Doubleday, 2005.

Hart, Joyce. *Frequently Asked Questions About Being Part of a Military Family.* New York, NY: Rosen Publishing, 2009.

Haerens, Margaret. *Veterans.* Farmington Hills, MI: Greenhaven, 2010.

Howe, Niamh Finlay. *So What, My Dad Has PTSD!* Raleigh, NC: Lulu, 2012.

Koontz, Christopher. *Enduring Voices: Oral Histories of the U.S. Army Experience in 2003–2005.* Washington, DC: U.S. Army, 2012.

McKay, Sharon E. *Thunder over Kandahar.* Toronto, ON, Canada: Annick Press, 2010.

Merino, Noel. *At Issue: U.S. Military Deployment.* Farmington Hills, MI: Greenhaven, 2010.

Nickelsberg, Robert. *Afghanistan: A Distant War.* New York, NY: Prestel USA, 2013.

Pasquini, Duke. *A Warrior's Son: A Teenage Son's Side of War.* Seattle, WA: CreateSpace, 2013.

Ritland, Michael, Gary Brozek, and Thea Feldman. *Navy SEAL Dogs: My Tale of Training Canines for Combat.* New York, NY: St. Martin's Griffin, 2013.

Sadler, Heather, ed. *Operation Trooplift: Postcards from Home.* Canberra, Australia: Odyssey, 2010.

Smithson, Ryan. *Ghosts of War: The True Story of a 19-Year-Old GI.* New York, NY: Harper Teen, 2014.

Underdahl, S. T. *No Man's Land.* Woodbury, MN: Flux, 2012.

U.S. Marine Corp. *Afghanistan: Alone and Afraid.* Washington, DC: U.S. Navy, 2010.

Wasdin, Howard E., and Stephen Templin. *I Am a SEAL Team Six Warrior: Memoirs of an American Soldier.* New York, NY: St. Martin's Press, 2012.

Wright, Darron. *Iraq Full Circle: From Shock and Awe to the Last Combat Patrol in Baghdad and Beyond.* Oxford, England: Osprey, 2012.

BIBLIOGRAPHY

American Fallen Soldiers Project. 2013. Retrieved February 14, 2014 (http://americanfallensoldiers.com).

Arlo, Rich. "Mt. Sinai Teen Helps Military Families with Swimming Lessons." Miller Place Rocky Point Patch, May 15, 2013. Retrieved January 9, 2014 (http://millerplace-rockypoint.patch.com/groups/volunteering/p/mount-sinai-teen-helps-military-families-with-swimming-lessons).

Blackman, Jeremy. "Teen Revamps Veterans Memorial Monument in Concord for Eagle Scout Project." *Concord Monitor*, May 28, 2013. Retrieved January 9, 2014 (http://www.concordmonitor.com/home/6386184-95/teen-revamps-veterans-memorial-monument-in-concord-for-eagle-scout-project).

Brennan, Thomas. "Lawn-Mowing Teen Wants to Help Wounded Vets," *Jacksonville Daily News*, April 29, 2013. Retrieved January 11, 2014 (http://www.newbernsj.com/news/military/lawn-mowing-teen-wants-to-help-wounded-vets-1.135036).

Cell Phones for Soldiers. "Cell Phones for Soldiers Celebrates 10 Years of Providing Precious Connections for Military Members." January 29, 2014. Retrieved March 6, 2014 (http://www.cellphonesforsoldiers.com).

Chandra, Anita, Sandraluz Lara Cinisomo, Lisa H. Jaycox, Terri Tanielian, Bing Han, Rachel M. Burns, and Teague Ruder. *Views from the Homefront: The Experiences of Youths and Spouses from Military Families.* Santa Monica, CA: RAND Corporation, 2011. Retrieved March 6, 2014 (http://www.rand.org/content/dam/rand/pubs/technical_reports/2011/RAND_TR913.pdf).

Conkey, Elizabeth. "Shaftsbury Teen Aids in Veterans Memorial Project." *Bennington Banner*, July 15, 2013. Retrieved January 11, 2014 (http://www.benningtonbanner.com/news/ci_23660431/shaftsbury-teen-aids-vet-memorial-project?-source=rss).

Create the Good. "Help Military Families." Retrieved February 23, 2014 (http://createthegood.org/toolkit/help-military-families/military-culture-tip-sheet).

Dog Tags for Kids. 2014. Retrieved February 23, 2014 (http://www.dogtagsforkids.com).

Fleming, Shauna. "A Million Thanks: How to Say Thank You to the Men and Women Serving Our Country." Retrieved March 6, 2014 (http://www.dosomething.org/project/a-million-thanks-how-say-thank-you-men-and-women-serving-our-country).

Help the Afghan Children. "The Benefits of Volunteering." Retrieved March 3, 2014 (http://www.helptheafghanchildren.org/pages.aspx?content=24).

Henry, Meghan, Alvaro Cortez, and Sean Morris. The 2013 Annual Homeless Assessment Report to Congress. Retrieved March 7, 2014 (https://www.onecpd.info/resources/documents/AHAR-2013-Part1.pdf).

Johnson and Wales University. "Community Service-Learning." Retrieved March 7, 2014 (https://www.jwu.edu/content.aspx?id=8916).

Massachusetts Department of Elementary and Secondary Education. "Service Learning: Promising Practices." June 16, 2011. Retrieved March 7, 2014 (http://www.doe.mass.edu/csl/program_profile.aspx?practice_id=125).

McCaughey, Frank. "Service Learning: Veterans and the Bronx." April 5, 2012. Retrieved February 3, 2014 (http://thenewlywedteacher.blogspot.com/2012/04/service-learning-veterans-and-bronx.html).

National Council for the Social Studies. "Curriculum Standards for Social Studies." Retrieved March 2, 2014 (http://www.mhschool.com/socialstudies/2009/teacher/pdf/ncss.pdf).

North Adams Public Schools. "Service Learning." Retrieved February 5, 2014 (http://drury.napsk12.org/service-learning-1).

Operation Kid Comfort. "Emily's Example of Dedicated Service." February 12, 2011. Retrieved January 12, 2014 (http://www.operationkidcomfort.blogspot.com).

Shayer, Joan. "Service Learning Project Helps Our Troops Call Home." *Ventura County Star*, April 11, 2009. Retrieved March 5, 2014 (http://www.vcstar.com/news/2009/apr/11/service-learning-project-helps-our-troops-call).

Stuffed Animals for Emergencies, Inc. "Donate Your Stuffed Animals to Our Military." Retrieved January 12, 2014 (http://www.stuffedanimalsforemergencies.org).

Teens Making a Difference. "Coupons for Military." Retrieved February 1, 2014 (http://teensmakingadifference.weebly.com/coupons-for-military.htmlhttp://teensmakingadifference.weebly.com/coupons-for-military.html).

U.S. Congress. United States Congressional Serial Set, Serial No. 14976, House Documents. Washington DC: U.S. Government Printing Office, 2006.

Document 77: Disabled American Veterans: Proceedings of 2005 annual convention, p. 28.

"Veterans Affairs Medical Center Youth Volunteer Receives $20,000 Scholarship." *Herald-Mail*, June 17, 2012. Retrieved January 12, 2014 (http://articles.herald-mail.com/2012-06-17/news/32285973_1_youth-volunteer-veterans-affairs-voluntary-service-scholarship-winner).

Vietnam Veterans Memorial Fund. "Hometown Heroes: A Service Learning Project." Retrieved March 7, 2014 (http://www.gailborden.info/bigread/images/pdf/HometownHeroesSLP.pdf).

Zimmerman, Beth. "Teen Gives All for Veterans and Pets." Pets for Patriots. Retrieved January 12, 2014 (http://blog.petsforpatriots.org/teen-gives-all-for-veterans-and-pets).

INDEX

A

AdoptaPlatoon, 5, 12
Afghanistan, 13, 25, 29
artists, 39, 46

B

bases, 6, 25, 27, 31, 35,
    36, 41

C

calling cards, 31, 48
curriculum standards, 8, 15

D

deployment,
    challenges of, 34–35
    help needed during, 23, 25,
        30–31, 34–37, 39–41, 61
disabilities, physical, 50
Dog Tags for Kids, 40
donations, 8, 10, 15, 16, 29,
    31, 46, 58
    in-kind, 14
DVDS4Vets, 26

H

Help the Afghan Children, 29
homelessness, 44, 50, 52
hospitals, veterans', 44, 47,
    48, 58
Hugs Project, 26, 27

I

Iraq, 4, 6, 8, 11, 12, 13, 15,
    19, 24, 27, 46, 59
Iraq and Afghanistan Veterans
    of America, 51

J

journals, 10, 17

L

letters, 4, 8, 13, 16, 21,
    23–25, 27, 31, 34, 38,
    47, 52

M

Magazines for Troops, 26
marines, 4, 6, 11, 24, 27, 36,
    37, 41, 55
Middle East, 8, 25
Million Thanks, A, 13, 24, 64

N

newsletter, school, 10, 52, 58

O

Operation Foot Care Patrol, 26
Operation Gratitude, 59
Operation Kid Comfort, 39
Operation Stand Down, 53–54

P

partners, 6, 12, 13, 16, 17, 21, 26, 28, 31, 33, 37, 39, 40, 42, 50, 52, 53, 55, 57, 58, 61
post-traumatic stress (PTS), 43, 50
Project Homefront, 61
projects, service learning
classroom, 5–6, 8, 54, 61
qualifications for, 11–12
results of, 6, 19

R

reports, 10, 52

S

safety, 6, 59
service learning,
benefits of, 12, 14, 62
definition of, 7
parts of, 10, 15, 16–17, 19, 21, 40, 42
purpose of, 7–8, 10–11
skills learned through, 8, 10, 12, 24–25, 29, 48
service, indirect, 39
soldiers
canine, 31, 33
hardships of, 13, 22, 24, 25, 43–44

items needed by, 23–24, 25–28
wounds of, 43, 59
Support Military Working Dogs, 33
Stuffed Animals for Emergencies, 4, 12

U

unemployment, 44, 50
U.S. Wardogs, 33

V

Vest-A-Dog, 33
Veterans Affairs, Department of (VA), 35, 44, 45, 48
Veterans History Project, 47–48
Vietnam Veterans Memorial Fund, 50–51
Vietnam War, 44, 50, 51
volunteers, 13, 39, 40, 44, 45, 61

W

wars, 4, 28
children affected by, 4–5 10, 12, 19, 57
loved ones lost to, 46, 50
soldiers' behavior affected by, 44
websites, 4, 13, 21, 42, 46, 58
Wounded Soldier's Wish, 13

ABOUT THE AUTHOR

Ann Byers is an educator and youth worker who lives in Fresno, California. The wife of a Vietnam-era veteran, she lives in an area proud of its strong military presence: a naval air station, an Army National Guard base, and a Veterans Administration hospital.

PHOTO CREDITS